This Faith Tremendous: Words of Ralph W. Loew

A sampling from the columns

Compiled by Maxine Uhl Loew

Express Press, Lima, Ohio

THIS FAITH TREMENDOUS

FIRST EDITION
Copyright © 1998 by
Ralph Loew

ISBN 0-7880-0954-0   PRINTED IN U.S.A.

Ralph W. Loew

This is our faith tremendous,
Our wild hope, who shall scorn,
That in the name of Jesus,
The world shall be reborn.

The words are adapted from a poem by Vachel Lindsay
written in praise of General Booth of the Salvation Army.
The Salvation Army has granted permission for their use
here.

Preface

Compiling this book has been a labor of love for me. These articles were written weekly for the daily newspaper. Because they dealt with issues and events that were happening at the moment, they do not naturally flow - one from another - as events in life don't seem to flow naturally, one from another.

I am happy to present these thoughts and musings of this gentle man of God in the hope that, here and there, they will meet your needs. Or, to quote grandson Jimmy, you'll "feel his hand on your shoulder."

Maxine Loew

Foreword

Ralph Loew was one of those very few people in the course of human history who cast a giant shadow across the life of a city, a region, a country. Ralph has left his unique imprint on the City of Buffalo, New York, and all of Western New York State.

Indeed, through his personal presence, his preaching and his writing, and through his outstanding efforts within his denomination and with the Chautauqua Institution, he has a significant impact on the lives of hundreds of thousands of people.

His fundamental love of humankind and his concern for the cares and misfortunes of others are evident in these articles, sermons, and essays. They are an expression of the enormous impact Ralph Loew had on the lives of so many. He was a truly remarkable person.

Daniel L. Bratton
Chautauqua Institution
Chautauqua, New York

Foreword

Opening a book, any book, is something like opening a package. If a package ticks, handle with care: it may explode in your face. Some books, like those written by the bearded god-killers named Marx, Darwin, Nietzsche, and Freud have done so in the face of millions. If a package gives off a pleasant odor, you may find peaches or apples, or a cracked perfume bottle inside. Some packages say "Handle With Care" or "This Side Up" or "Do Not Open Until Christmas." Many of them spell out directions for how to open them and how to use what is inside. A certain sense of mystery, an occasion for surprise, accompanies many packages, while others are quite predictable and inspire ho-hums.

This Faith Tremendous is a package that opens up to several dozen short reflections, spiritual essays on an astonishing variety of themes tied together thanks to the consistency of the person who penned them, the late pastor, friend, entrepreneur, and citizen Ralph Loew.

The book does not "tick" with the threat of explosion, but it can effect change in the reader. The only aroma is that of newly cut paper and a newly glued spine, but whoever figuratively breathes in while reading will find pleasure. "Handle with Care"? Yes, if you do not want to be inspired or changed or forced to look at things differently. "This Side Up"? My hunch is that it will be read by people prone in bed or crunched on planes, bent at desks or while walking the treadmill or pedaling the stationary bicycle. From whatever posture or direction, it should help "right" one. "Do Not Open Until..?" Some of the little essays are seasonal, but they can be enjoyed in all seasons.

So we come to "Directions." My advice is: "Take One a Day." Let Loew work on you. Read early in the morning and let it help set a tone for the day. If an Easter essay hits you on July 4, fine; every day was (and is) Easter to Pastor Loew. If it happens to deal with Christmas on an April day, why not let Christmas past and future meet on a spring morning, when the idea that God lives among us is not hard to sustain. If a prose poem says "1967" and you are reading it a third of a century later, let the historical frame serve to present a picture of enduring themes.

This package might have been called "post-modern," a concept that one does not need to understand Ralph Loew. It would probably have been dismissed with a polite and never cruel sneer or snort, but a sneer or snort nontheless, for the author, who was never afraid of change, was quite dismissive of fads. But if the post-modern implies, as it does in visual art, something of the pastiche, of the assemblage or montage or collage, this book has that element. Open it and immediately you are plunged into a Commencement Day. No page turned prepares you for what to expect on the next page to be turned. Yet the total package works its effect.

What makes this varied collection work for coherence is the fact that its author was someone who knew himself and his God, who knew what he wanted to say, and what he hoped you'd hear. It is the voice of Ralph Loew the pastor, who faithfully tended a flock through decades of change in Buffalo. To that pastorate he added many interests, but not other vocations. One could stroll a path at the Chautauqua Institution with him, or, just as likely hurry along because he had a program to produce, and find him interrupted by virtual or total strangers who knew of him by reputation, recognized his face, and had something to ask him. Protestant, Catholic, Jew, nonbeliever - these are brand names for the people and peoples in downtown Buffalo or at table at Chautauqua; it mattered not. They could confide, Loew could listen, and then impart. These essays reflect the spirit of such impartations.

That pastoral, which means shepherding, sense colored his role as citizen in Buffalo. The years of his pastorate were not easy for that city, which suffered blizzards that alienated the sunbirds, demographic including racial change that led many to desert or to give up on the downtown that has to be the heart of a city. Ralph Loew could be heartsick over some of the disasters: the invasion of drug culturists, the increase of crime in the street, the trashing of fine arts by people who had no taste or ear for a symphony, the desertion by many of municipal responsibilities, intolerance. But heartsickness never let him succumb to despair. His faith, his philosophy, his family and friends helped him rally against and counter many of the bad forces during the half century of his prime. And that fight-back spirit shows in these never-"down" little essays.

More than most busy pastors and citizens, Ralph Loew remained intellectually curious. These short chapters, with their occasional references to the Niebuhrs, the Lippmanns, the Weils, are little vivid evidences of his wide and persistent reading. No one expects a book of this sort to develop in detail insights he garnered from his reading. But Loew had a gift for finding the nugget, the nub, the core of an idea in a short quotation and then setting it forth for new readerships in new contexts.

Ralph Loew the friend comes through in the package that *This Faith Tremendous* turns out to be. He had the gift and grace of Maxine at his side through all the years of his adulthood and ministry, and anyone who knows her, the compiler of this book, has some sense of why he was able to look forward to the future with hope and to guide others to hope. The Loew house, for those of us fortunate to have been there, was pleasantly crowded with memorabilia, souvenirs, awards - all of them there to help the Loew's keep in mind good things that had happened to them along the trail or to give evidence that others appreciated the Loew endeavors. Yet, impressively, there as on these pages we do not confront an egocentric, strutting cleric of the sort that turns so many off. There is almost a boyish wonder on these pages: look at the graces, the gifts, the opportunities we have along life's way, he would be shouting had he not chosen conversational tones as he wrote.

My own ties to the author go back to the 1960s when he trusted me as a young person to represent our faith in mixed forums in Buffalo, or to present ideas about religion in the mix of Chautauqua, down to the time when I got to preach in the congregation where he was by then emeritus. Like everyone else to whom I've ever talked who had dealings with Ralph, I came away richer for the experience, as I did once more when reading these modest leavings from his storehouse.

Let me close with a word about the interfaith dimension of his life work. I doubt whether there is a line on these pages that would do anything but speak to a Catholic who comes obliquely to the work of this Lutheran, a Protestant. Loew was "born ecumenical." Jews, Muslims, people of Asian religious traditions, who will find that his expounding of specifically Christian themes such as the resurrection of Jesus Christ alien, will stand at some distance when those focal points come up. The faiths *are* different, and Pastor Loew never pretended otherwise. But the otherbelievers and the nonbelievers who found him such a clear and congenial conversationalist and expounder at Chantauqua or on his many travels, can be assured that here, in rniniature, they are getting a very clear picture of what Christian faith is supposed to do for someone in both personal and public life. By analogy, they can carry away elements of faith and hope and love that can inform their lives, as they are on different paths. And in learning what made Loew "tick," they will have in their hands indeed a creatively explosive little package.

Now it's time for me to get out of the way and to let him commence by taking us to a Commencement and then to a leisurely tour of places and ideas through essays that will last long after they were first written and beyond the lift of this book. Too many have been changed by their encounter with Ralph Loew to let his influence be confined. If you are an old friend, the book will provide you with reasons for recall. If you are a newcomer to his lore, I am sure he would want me to say "Welcome."

Martin E. Marty
Fairfax M. Cone Distinguished Service Professor at the University of Chicago, and long-time F.O.L. (friend of Loews')

Chapter I. My Lord, and My God

- **From the first column in this section, We Are Wanted: Mankind:**
  Mankind yearns for that one fixed point, a center, something stable that can be counted on. And he wants that not to be a figment of his own yearning or a concoction growing from from his need.

- **From The Miracle of Easter, the last column in this section:**
  Life is not just breathing one breath after another,
      ticking off an existence by counting the years.
  Easter is the faith that life needs not be limited by
      time and space.

We Are Wanted

These are the days of Elgar's "Pomp and Circumstance," the stately processionals, the dignified seniors, proud parents, and concerned young families. These are the days of the graduates. Suddenly young persons are aware that some major influences have brought them to this achievement, shaping their ideas, giving form to their philosophy, setting something of the pace for the future.

At one college convocation the speaker asked the 3,000 graduates from the various schools of disciplines to stand up. They did. Then he asked them to be seated. They were. At which time he is reported to have pointed out how quickly they obeyed his words and how susceptible they are to words and influences that are barraging them every day.

The poet Auden once wrote of youth as that area of life just waiting anxiously for something to happen:

> ...to be young means
> To be all on edge, to be held waiting in
> A packed lounge for a personal call
> From Long Distance, for the low voice that
> Defines one's future. The fears we know
> Are of not knowing. Will nightfall bring us
> Some awful order... Keep a hardware store
> In a small town... Teach science for life to
> Progressive girls? It is getting late.
> Shall we ever be asked for? Are we simply
> Not wanted at all?

Under the dignified composure of the graduation day there are also anxieties that torture the mind. It is at this point that all of us search for a hitching post in the universe. **Mankind yearns for that one fixed point, a center, something stable that can be counted on. And he wants that not to be a figment of his own yearning or a concoction growing from his need.**

Faith Is Our Home

Some years ago the family of an architect confronted the problem of living in various places of the world and still keeping something of a sense of home. His wife and daughter knew that they would be living for three months or a year in some foreign city and then would be off to another area. It sounded glamorous to the stay-at-home relatives; to this family it posed a problem: **What and where was home?**

They decided to take one article with them, an alabaster bust of a young woman. It was one of those pieces of elegance that frequently graced homes in a more Victorian age. Now, whenever this family came into a hotel in Rome or in an apartment in Algeria, the first box opened was the piece of alabaster. When the bust was unpacked and placed on a mantelpiece or table, the family was at home.

More and more the problem confronted by this family is our common problem. Families move not once but five and six times in the short period of a decade. The social consequences of this kind of disruption have not been adequately measured. The provincial qualities of the old villages, redolent with such insights as *Winesburg, Ohio*, are lost in the new villages called suburbs where many only "tent overnight."

If home were established as easily as unpacking a familiar symbol, it would be an easy problem to solve. It's more subtle. **Home is where nothing can separate a person from his intrinsic worth.**

Robert Frost knew its meaning when he wrote:

> Home is the place where, when you have to go there,
> They have to take you in.
> I should have called it
> Something you somehow haven't to deserve.

And the ancient psalmist in a time of nomadic wanderers knew this consciousness of at-homeness, confessing:

> Lord, thou hast been our dwelling place in all generations.

The haunting questions nag us. In this universe, what do we carry with us? An ancient ark? A piece of marble? A nostalgic memory? Or a faith that is more portable?

Perhaps our greatest need is to be at home with ourselves. There is a gnawing ache in too many lives, a sense of purposelessness, the old unforgiven sin and the dull agony which calls for something or someone and no one seems to answer back.

We are free from many of the old restraints and the old ties which held us in more provincial times. Now we have to learn that inner discipline of a new at-homeness. This is far more than adapting ourselves to our environment.

To be at home with God is to understand that the human being has an inner residence, "something you haven't to deserve." We need this now - and if we travel to the moon we'll need it all the more.

The Cross Says: God Loves Me Now

This is the story of a man who used a bent nail to keep his sanity.

During the Nazi madness, many people suffered because of their faith, among them a bishop of the Lutheran Church named Hans Lilje. Dr. Lilje discovered himself in a cell, devoid of every comfort, windowless except for a slit high on one wall. Not only were the prisoners stripped of their familiar possessions, but their jailers also tortured them with a kind of horror by attempting to confuse their sense of time. Dates, the days of the week and the identifying familiarity of time were blotted out. Monday was called Thursday and Tuesday became Saturday. Yet when Sunday came, even when the jailers denied the day, the bishop would call out verses of Scripture and lead his fellow-prisoners in singing some ancient chorale.

What the guards had overlooked in their tactics was simply a bent nail. The bishop had used it to draw a circle on the dirt-covered floor. He had drawn a circle divided into seven sections, and when a ray of morning light fought its fitful way through the little slit at the top of the wall, he moved his strange "sun dial" to a new day. It was a little thing, a method of defiance. More than this, it became a way by which these prisoners could hang on to a sense of dignity.

A Cross, high and lifted up, may seem to be a very weak weapon with which to do battle with today's demoniac forces. It is a lifeline of Lent that this same cross can help man to remember his true worth. We live in a time when the tactics of the enemy are to strip man of his meaning. The added problem is that our own gadgets do the same. Our very success poses a threat. Suppose that our economy becomes tied completely to our missiles. Suppose that our automation strips us of our desire for excellence and craftsmanship. In such a time as this, what can help us to discover the time of day? All too many of us are acquainted with the individual who has come to middle life, has achieved success, and yet doesn't seem to know what time it is. He doubts the very worth of his own achievements.

In such a world, the cross of Christ stands as the reminder of a deliberate choice of one who refused to barter his soul for comfort, or his goals for security. He wrestled out the problem, for it wasn't an easy choice. His was not the choice to die. It was rather the choice to proclaim the gospel of love. If that brought him into conflict with the forces of his time, then he would die rather than forsake that kingdom. So his broken body on a cross becomes a kind of bent nail for mankind.

Jesus once told a story of a boy who demanded his inheritance, got it, and went off to have a time of hilarity. When his wealth was gone, he had a multitude of jobs, ending as the keeper of a pigsty. There, St. Luke states, this boy "came to himself." It was at that moment he decided to go home. He felt he had no right to be his father's son and his father had to remind him that he had always been his son.

Many of us may not feel redeemable, yet the cross reminds us that man is worth saving.

Anything that degrades man, strips him of meaning, uses him as a tool, enslaves him to false habits, and distorts his image of himself is a nail in a cross.

Anything that reminds man of his essential worth, enables him to express love for his neighbor, calls him to a sense of personal responsibility and relates him to the fact that God loves him is a bent nail which reminds him that he is a child of God. The cross is a fact which may help us to come to ourselves, challenging us to become what we already are, persons made in the image of God.

Beyond The Tomb

EASTER

is the assurance that life is more than a battle for survival. Wars occur, truth is degraded, hopes are destroyed, and yet something else is happening:
This is the assurance that there is a life and truth which cannot be destroyed.

EASTER

is the knowledge that God is always dealing with our situation. Just when we think that the tombs are permanent, there is the rush of new life. Just when we had centered all of our attention on ourselves and our own acts, **His reality astonishes us with His presence.**

EASTER

is this assurance of new meanings for our present, because there is Reality at the end of the road.

Faith vs. Doubt

Easter is past, and we remember those who had - and have - their doubts. **What does a man do with his doubts? In this world of rapidly changing ideas, some of the old words don't have the same emotional pull.** So a man begins to doubt. What then?

Such a one is the central figure in a novel, *The Martyred*, by Richard Kim. This story of martyred Korean pastors and of the two who were not killed is a drama of a contemporary Job. Here are torturing doubts, unrelenting tragedies, and the searching for the truth as though these were waves breaking against the fact of Easter.

One man, refusing to bend beneath his doubts, yet never quite believing, could plead, "We must fight despair, we must destroy it and not let the slickness of despair corrupt the life of man and reduce him to a mere scarecrow."

So one man takes his doubts and wears them as though they were a crown. He was hoping against hopelessness.

Yet the answer to doubt is not this kind of hoping; it is another kind of seeing, or recognition, and experience. It is acknowledging that one does not know everything before one can act.

- Centuries ago men thought that God wanted them to annihilate the enemy;

There came another who doubted this and talked of a God of love.

- Centuries ago men talked of the subjugation of various races as being inferior;

There came those who doubted this and brought a new understanding of our humanity and our godly dignity.

- Centuries ago there were those who thought you could keep God in one spot, run out on Him - even entomb Him;

There came the doubters who discovered that you cannot elude the presence of God.

Honest doubts never stand still; they move to a new kind of faith! It was a new faith that spoke of the God of love, that understood the dignity of man made in the image of God, that understood the loving presence of God.

The problem of doubt is that faith could be ruled out as a possibility. This is always the most disturbing situation to confront after Easter. Simone Weil, the French mystic, has written,

> The danger is not lest the soul should doubt where there is any bread, but lest, by a lie, it should persuade itself that it is not hungry.

The Korean pastor said, "We must dare to hope against despair because we are men."

It would be better if we would hope against despair because we know that God is there, even when we have not understood that presence.

Easter presents a continuing search, a faith that, beyond the despair, there is a very certain reality!

The Wisdom of Faith

There is a famous prayer that can be uplifted each day:

**Lord, give me the serenity to accept what cannot be changed,
Give me the courage to change what ought to be changed,
And the wisdom to know the difference.**

Attributed to the eminent theologian, Dr. Reinhold Niebuhr, this prayer opens life to those twins of serenity and courage that merge into wisdom.

Any one of us has an inventory of personal or social problems to demand both this serenity and the courage. At the risk of oversimplification, here are a few:

"Lord, give me the serenity to accept" ...The difficult fact of myself.

That's a demanding discipline. Too many persons live through their lives without ever really actually making their faith articulate. The guilt-ridden can't forgive themselves; and the cynical won't even confront themselves.

"Lord give me the serenity to accept"... Today.

Many persons who are unwilling to be seen in last year's clothing continue to wear last century's values. Only those who have the serenity to accept the fact that they live in the "Now" can claim the grace to live serenely in the most demanding of circumstances.

"Lord give me the grace to accept"... God.

In a time of scientific acceleration and knowledge-explosion, our ideas of God may have been too small. He is greater than our ideas. To accept God is to understand that a man can know the power of God which creates the godly.

"Give me the courage to change"... Apathy.

That sin which permits men to get accustomed to ugliness, to corruption, or to a divided humanity is the yawn of the cynic. In every town there is a need to pray for the courage to rout apathy.

"Give me the courage to change"... Hopelessness.

In an age of many things there is also the loss of pride in craftsmanship. Too many are willing to settle for getting by instead of knowing the inner drive which demands the yearning for excellence When great reverences are treated casually, there is an air of hopelessness which settles on the human race.

"Give me the courage to change"... Fear.

It's a strange fear that immobilizes so many. John Ciardi once said: "We are so afraid of going broke that we're afraid to go for broke."

"And the wisdom to know the difference"...

That's the faith and trust that enables a man to know that nothing can separate him from the love of God.

Either we are tools of the Almighty or we are pawns of the dreadful. Today we pray for this God-given serenity, courage, and wisdom.

The Miracle of Easter

A young Hungarian stood before an international assemblage
and quietly spoke three words.

He had come through danger and tyranny. His voice had the
ring of Easter as he said,

"We are alive."

The miracle of Easter is this quiet recognition
That mankind is meant for life.
Life is not just breathing one breath after another,
Ticking off an existence by counting the years.
Easter is the faith that life need not be limited
by time and space. There is a new
significance to our "now."
The steeples of the churches constantly point
to this fact: the Easter faith is in no
earthly permanence.
The world is filled with tombs that are sealed by
the heavy stones of prejudice and hatred.
Think what would happen to these tombs if
there were a rush of adventurous action
filled with Easter hope.
For we are not the slaves of death. **We are alive!**

Chapter II. Possess What You Own

> - **From the first column in this section, Have You an Identity:**
>   That person has really come to himself who knows that he is a part of the familyhood of God and is free to live like it.
> - **From the last column in this section, The World Needs "Easter Christians":**
>   Life is not a camera that smashes into the craters of death. Easter proclaims that life can be met with courage and death with dignity.

Have You an Identity?

"Identify yourself!" That's the command of the guard at the border of the country. It's the polite question of the passport officer. It's the querulous request of the banker who wonders about your check. It's the common question as a man gives his assurance of his reputation as well as of his existence.

A whole host of causes have indicated the need modern man has in finding this identification in something beyond his own situation. From civil rights to Peace Corps, from the gyrating Beatlemaniac to the dedicated scientist, men have identified themselves with a cause in which they can lose themselves.

The search for personhood is more than joining a group or wearing a name bracelet. It's more than a badge or an identity card. It is the ability to become an organized, effective and creative person, one who has found himself not as a notorious person or a personality-cult or as a publicity seeker. That's why finding self is always losing self.

There are three simple stories in the Bible which ought to be retold in these difficult and exciting days:

- There was a shepherd who noticed the loss of one sheep, so he hunted until he had found it and restored it to the flock. He gave identity to the sheep.
- There was a woman who lost a coin - really a part of her dowry, as though she had lost the diamond from her engagement ring. She hunted in every dark corner until she found it and restored it to its rightful place. She gave it identity.

- There was a father who waited for his wayward son despite that rascal's insistence on wasting his inheritance. Having lost all, the son came to himself and returned to be his father's servant. When he arrived home, his father restored him to the family circle. He renewed the son's identity.

This is the primary importance of real religion. It is the winning of persons to the realization of that which they already are. The sheep was already a part of the flock, the son was already a member of the family. That had to be restated and recovered.

A casual look around any neighborhood can emphasize the number of persons who have either lost identity or are trying to deny it to others.

In a world which is all too often impersonal, it is important to lose one's self in the right cause. The stakes are high. Some people manage to elude the question for all too long a time but ultimately there is the command:

"Identify yourself."

That person has really come to himself who knows that he is a part of the familyhood of God and is free to live like it.

Possess What You Own

Not long ago a little lady in our city died. There were no immediate heirs, and there were few persons who knew her well. She had lived to herself, dressing in severe and threadbare clothes, eating from cracked dishes, and spending little. Yet the executor of the will discovered expensive china, silver service, and a considerable amount of money which had been hoarded for some rainy day. The lady owned much; she possessed nothing.

Frederick Lewis Allen tells of the financial tycoon, J. Pierpont Morgan, seated in his study on Madison Avenue surrounded by first editions of the world's finest literature. His library was a treasure, but Mr. Morgan seldom read his books and was more content to sit by the fireplace playing solitaire. He owned much; he possessed so little.

We have lamented the immorality of so many acts that we fail to discover the immorality of our failure to act. Our non-use of our opportunities becomes the tragedy. A recent study of the moral crisis of our own time recounted the wastage of talent and the missed opportunities.

Here is the story of the young man who has an I.Q. of almost 200 who refuses to give himself to any project, vegetating instead of being spent. This is the immorality of apathy which must be confronted by every one of us.

- It is one thing to own a violin; it is another thing to possess the ability to play it with freedom.
- It is one thing to own a book; it is another thing to read it with understanding.
- It is one thing to own a ticket to travel; it is another thing to possess the ability to understand what one sees and appreciate what one experiences.

- It is one thing to own one's freedom; it is another thing to act with that delicious joy that comes to those who move with the security of responsible liberty.

> O I could sing such grandeur and glories about you:
> You have not known what you are, you have slumbered upon yourself all your life
> The mockeries are not you!
> Underneath them and with them I see you lurk.
> Whatever you are, claim your own.

So challenged Walt Whitman and once more it's the demand to possess what we own.

Possession is more than nine-tenths of the law; possession is one hundred percent of love. It is loving the possibility of life to avoid hiding a light under a bushel, burying a talent, or withdrawing from life.

St. Paul insisted that those who were really the workers with God might have nothing yet they possess all things.

When men measure the worth of their fellows they are liable to ask, "How much does he own?" They might add to it, "How does he use what he owns?"

The true measure of a person is known in his ability to possess what he owns!

The Bible and Understanding

Some few years ago two men were riding the train from Moscow to Paris. In this European compartment six persons sat staring at one another. Of these six, one was a Russian who was reading a little book. As the rough but somewhat rhythmic motion of the train assaulted his body, he began to be sleepy, dozed, and the book slipped from his hands to the floor. Across from him sat a Frenchman who retrieved the book and then recognized that it was a Bible.

He couldn't speak Russian nor could he read the language but the markings were unmistakable. Quickly he reached into his duffel bag on the ledge above and brought out his own Bible. Returning the first book to the now awake Russian, he pointed to his French version. He opened to the 23rd Psalm. The Russian did likewise. They read and they smiled. The Russian pointed to the 13th Chapter of First Corinthians. The Frenchman did the same. In this fashion they communicated with one another, spending hours reading without speaking, conversing without sharing one another's language.

This little story of Andre Rosser is a parable of our contemporary need. Everywhere we've lost communication. Parents lose it with their children. Neighbors lose it with other neighbors. Mobs threaten embassies, wars are prophesied, and angry words are shouted. We stare at one another or glower at one another while the train of circumstances jostles us against one another.

With our communications broken, can we find a common treasure through which we can find an understanding and a common search for truth?

Our problem in our personal lives as well as in our families and in our communities is that we have lost the Bible from our duffel bag, or from the consciousness of our everyday life. We are in danger of making of our religion a "public ceremony," a kind of gesture or salute, something which is nice and pious but empty.

The death of religion as a means of communication occurs when that happens:

- In the rash of new movies concerning the Bible and the life of Christ, will you be able to spot the liberties which have been taken by those who thought that they could improve upon the story?

- When a person says - sometimes glibly "All that we need is the Sermon on the Mount," will you be able to agree in a knowledgeable way? Could you ask him what it is in that sermon which could create the possibility of new relationships just now?

We are all on the journey of life and the communications are breaking down. Somewhere we need to find in our minds, or in the luggage of our journey, the source material for understanding which outleaps our language problems, our agonies of conflict and our troubled emptiness.

Being Too Busy Poor Excuse For Missing Life

How busy? - The father of four youngsters was explaining his schedules to me the other evening. Said he, "They're little now and I find myself very busy. Frankly, I don't find children very stimulating. But they'll be getting into their teens one of these times and then I shall look forward to some companionship with them."

It might have been dismissed as the unthinking statement of a person who has no awareness of life - except that the speaker was a professional man with several degrees after his name.

He is gone! - He should meet a prophet of the Old Testament who was having difficulty in making an appointment with the King. So he disguised himself as a veteran of the battles and told the King a story of a guard who had been charged with the care of a prisoner. However, the prisoner had escaped and the guard's only excuse was, "As I was busy here and there, he was gone." The King said that it was obvious how to deal with such a guard. Whereupon the prophet tore off his disguise and charged the King with the kind of busyness that degraded his kingdom.

They won't wait - This is at the heart of our complicated problem in modern living. We are likely to allow the things that matter most to be at the mercy of the things that matter least. Our busyness may be important. Or it just may be our unhappy attempt to prove something to ourselves.

Waiting to talk to the children until they get to be teenagers will be a long, long wait for my friend. He will discover that his children do not know him and do not want to talk to him. While he is busy, they are gone.

NOW is the time –
- Here is the man who is too busy to read and wants to wait until he has retired. He will not know how to read.
- Here is the woman who would like to hear good music but will wait until there are quiet hours. She will not know how to listen.
- Here is the family that will wait until it suits its convenience to go to church. Its members will discover that while they were busy, they had missed the sustaining wonder of worship.

No excuse - The fact that we are busy is no excuse for having lost a sense of responsibility for life. It might even occur to us that we are not the first people in the world to be busy.

As a matter of fact, I have just read recently that Bach had to compose a cantata for every Sunday as well as to teach his pupils. He was busy. And Luther said once that he was so busy one day that he had to pray for three hours before starting. They were busy.

Don't remind me that these people were geniuses. Then the mark of genius is the ability to be concerned with what matters most, despite the demands of schedule.

While we are busy – There is much truth in the comment reported by J. B. Priestley:

Chesterton once shrewdly observed that there was a great difference between an eager man who wanted to read a book and a tired man who wanted a book to read. We have too many tired persons who merely want a book to read, a program to listen to, and to be smothered in stuffy comfort while they are doing it.

He might have added that in our tiredness we have missed the glory of talking with a child, sharing something meaningful with the family, or refreshing the inner resources of the person.

One thing is certain: there is a difference between those two statements -

"While I was busy, he was gone." and

"I was so busy that I had to pray for three hours."

Understanding this difference is learning how to live.

Guard the Rosebush

Some years ago Walter Lippmann recounted the story of one of the last czars of Russia who came upon a sentry guarding a patch of weeds. He retraced his steps a few days later and spied the sentry at the same spot. The sentry did not know why he was there or what he was guarding. The captain of the guards did not know. No one knew.

Since the czar was a czar, he ordered a thorough research of the problem. Ultimately it was revealed that almost a century before, Catherine the Great had planted a rosebush at that spot. Not wanting it to be trampled she had ordered the guard. The rosebush died but no one remembered to cancel the sentry duty. History had come sweeping by. But still the sentry stood at attention by the weed patch.

Lippmann commented upon the story saying,
It is always difficult to know that a rosebush is dead and that you are guarding an empty place. This is particularly true of the hopes and fears which sweep across the modern world and for a time possess men's minds and govern their conduct.

Or change the metaphor. In a delightful little book which interprets some of the theological implications of the cartoon "Peanuts," the cartoonist, Mr. Schultz, discusses the obsession of Linus with his blanket:

Linus' affection for his blanket is a symbol of the things we cling to. What I am getting at, of course, is the adult's inability to give up habits which really should be given up.

Not that I am completely against the idea that we have to cling to something. For once you accept Jesus, it does not mean that all your problems are automatically

39

solved or that you will never be lonesome or unhappy again. How can you be happy all of the time if you are aware of the things that are going on around you? But some of the adult habits are ridiculous.

So the child who interprets happiness as a thumb and a blanket can become a man who still clings to an emotional satisfaction which is somewhat meaningless.

With these stories in mind, range the areas of debates in our cities and villages today. Many times the battle is over the wrong cause. Somebody is guarding the weed patch instead of the rosebush. Someone is clinging to the "thumb and blanket" when they ought to be confronting the real issues unafraid.

If we die for the wrong causes or hide behind some meaningless sentimentality, we'll fragment the forces for good instead of meeting the problems which beset us.

It's no time to guard an empty place. It's no time to panic. It is a time to plant the rosebushes. It is a time to be certain that we aren't clinging to some old symbol of security instead of finding that delicious inner security of the unafraid.

The stories of the Old and New Testaments are filled with the active verbs of men and women who marched, tackled great issues, and kept their eyes on the things that mattered most. In testing times someone may have to stand guard over the rosebush. Let's make certain it's there!

The Eternal Values

Spring and summer fashions are advertised everywhere. The cut of the brim or the slant of the lapel, the hem of the skirt or the clothes that cover or don't - all of them are important. St. Paul said that "the fashions of the world pass away," but most persons are inclined to listen to the 17th century author who said, "As good be out of the world as out of fashion."

Now the matter is far more important than the fashions of the moment. A foundation recently appropriated enormous sums of money in order to retrain engineers who had been away from college for a decade. This is an effort to keep these highly skilled men from becoming obsolescent. Technical science moves so rapidly that it becomes necessary to know what is happening tomorrow in order to understand today.

But the paradox is simply that we understand the need in technical skills and ignore it in human relations. Think of the numbers of citizens who are willing to espouse 1864 ethics in regard to racial tensions while they live in 1964! These aren't the days of Uncle Tom and the Civil War. We ought to keep up-to-date!

So a person who would not be caught in public with last years dress may mouth an idea which is hopelessly antiquated! Too many of us talk about the good old days without wanting to bring any of the "goodness" of those days into the present.

Eternal values are always contemporary, alive in the present as well as the past. That's why they are "eternal."

Jesus insisted that heaven and earth would pass away as surely as last year's fashions, but he also emphasized that the word of God would not pass away. It was the old idea; it was the new situation.

It was the eternal principle; it was the contemporary understanding.

It's about time to keep up-to-date in our human relations. Events outstrip our understanding and suddenly our own situation reveals our moral bankruptcy.

New occasions teach new duties;

Time makes ancient good uncouth; They must upward still and onward

Who would keep abreast of truth.

There is an eternal truth; we need to know that in terms of today. We need to keep up-to-date with a God of our present instead of worshiping the outgrown practices of another time.

The World Needs Easter Christians

Stand at the Berlin Wall and stare at the crooked guarded entrances, the menacing guards, and the sealed border. To breach the wall seems impossible. To attempt it seems incredible. Yet the young man speaking with us had come through that wall!

Talk to some neighbors who normally are gentle and cultured but who, from time to time, share harsh attitudes about human relations. To break down that wall seems impractical and impossible. Yet there is a new spirit at work and the new breakthroughs are obvious. Ideas had breached the wall.

These are events in our time. Easter marks the event in another time that breaks into our time. Some men had seen their friend die on the Cross. They were paralyzed with fright and frustration. Yet within days they were out on the highways with the bold word of undefeated life. They had faith that he had broken the sealed tomb. Easter had breached the wall.

Our world needs Easter Christians. We've chided these people who crowd the churches in an annual pilgrimage. Suppose they didn't come - even on Easter. Suppose that there was no one to share the word that there had been a breakthrough of the wall of fear and suspicion.

The real Easter Christian is the undefeated believer who refuses to accept the verdict of death to men's hopes. Even a "once-a-year" tradition admits this; there's the chance that the gesture could become a commitment!

The mystery of life beyond the grave is as real today as it was in times past. Easter is the assurance that man can refuse to make the tomb his horizon and death his goal. **Life is not a camera that smashes into the craters of death. Easter proclaims that life can be met with courage and death with dignity**. It is the refusal to be walled in.

Stand at any bristling wall in this angry world. The walls are everywhere. You'll always find the cynical, or the defeated, or the fear-paralyzed.

Yet you'll always find the undefeated, the hopeful and the persistent lovers of righteousness. They're the real Easter Christians. They refuse to take a wall - or a sealed tomb - as the final verdict.

Chapter III. A New Way: "But I Say Unto You..."

- **From the first column in this section, Light For Murky Waters:**
  Immediately he kicks up mud and is lost in a cloud which he himself has aroused.
- **From the last column in this section, Fragility of Human Defenses:**
  It is the fragility of our defense that is so disturbing ... Too many of us have been content to think of our safety in terms of the vulnerable building of our own possessions.

Light for Murky Waters

We were flying at an altitude of 15,000 feet, and talking about life at the bottom of the ocean. My seatmate was a distinguished scientist whose technical skills are assisting in the development of the possibilities of underwater exploration.

He told of the problems of breathing, the necessity of understanding the strange underwater sounds, and the enormous challenges of the pressure of the sea. Among other problems he recounted the dilemma of the pioneer who ventures from his protective capsule. **Garbed in his strange sea costume, he starts out to explore the ocean depths, searching for new oil reserves and minerals, or just making surveys of the ancient topography. Immediately he kicks up mud and is lost in a cloud which he himself has aroused.**

The situation is a vivid one. We can consider all the angry turmoil stirred into blackness by our own endeavors. The man at the bottom of the ocean will be protected by a kind of radar device which sends out sound waves, and "sees" for the man who is able to understand the pattern. Suppose that we had such a moral sound wave or a clear sense of what we call God's providence?

It's this which the ancients discussed in their search for a way of life. A casual reading of these events in Scripture would seem to indicate that these worthies thought of God as a kind of divine sound ray, keeping them out of scrapes and difficulties.

This is true only when we understand that in all of their dreams and visions, God was sending them back to their tasks.

Read your Bible and you are impressed with the fact that these persons were never delivered from dealing with the problem. This wasn't any "pie in the sky" kind of religion. It sent the ancient prophets and their later counterparts into the battle. They dealt with all of the muddied situations. They had that inner courage to do what they believed God wanted them to do.

Our prayers are not for escape, but for light. Our hopes are not only for deliverance, but for guidance. Our faith is not to dodge the fact that these are tough problems; our faith is the assurance that these tough problems can be solved, that we can see through the muddy waters, that we can find our way.

Science may make it possible for us to build a kind of city at the bottom of the ocean. Faith in the God of us all can still make it possible for us to build a city of righteousness on the surface of this planet. We need the knowledge of that guidance, even as we explore the moon and our own seas' depths.

Unshakable Fact

It must have been a dramatic moment for one knowledgeable scientist who had gone to church on Good Friday. The city was Seattle. Observing the traditional rites of a sacred day, this worshiper looked up from his prayers and noted that the chandelier in the great cathedral was shaking violently. He left the church, hurried to his instruments and verified the fact that is now known to the world - Alaska was suffering a devastating earthquake.

But what of the others who saw the chandelier shake? Some might have wondered what was happening. Some said, "That's odd." Some thought, "There must be a loose connection which should be repaired."

When the chandelier shook, some never noticed at all. The ancient prophets were certain that God was shaking the earth. Jeremiah described the horror of the earthquake and insisted,

> I look out... and lo, the sown land lies a desert;
> And the towns are razed by the Lord's rage.

Isaiah was as certain that there was more to the earthquake than the shifting of the deeps. He felt the shaking and wrote,

> The foundations of the earth do shake.
> Earth splits to pieces,
> Earth is split into pieces,
> Earth shakes to pieces,
> Earth reels like a drunken man,
> Earth rocks like a hammock.

But he added to this vivid description of the earthquake his insistence that all of this was happening because of the weight of earth's own transgression. Everything you could touch was shaking. Yet he saw a Fact unshaken.

It is at this point that modern man senses his dilemma. He can measure the earthquakes. He knows what is happening. Yet he has not been able to develop the kind of moral seismograph which can measure the tremors in his personal conduct, the moral shifting in the earth, the rumbles which might be the prelude to a terrible devastation. After the wars or after the knowledge of the murder of millions, he understands that this was a devastation. But in the midst of his present situation, he understands only that some chandeliers are shaking and he doesn't know what to do about it. Sometimes he manages not to notice.

What are the facts that are not shaken? If we have illiteracy about the deeps of our own selves, no wonder there is a silence before the injustices and the loss of reverence and the lack of courage. It is not a time to shake ones head and wonder what's happening. It is the time to act with the certainty that there is a Lord who still says, The world itself shall crumble, but my salvation knows no end!

Have Faith in Change

Very few people enjoy change. To move from one city to another can be a major crisis. The change of jobs necessitating new skills or habits can shatter the ease with which one formerly tackled the daily round.

The greatest change every person has to confront may not necessarily be change of house, or of geographical situation or of job. It is simply to change one's mind.

That can be a shattering experience. For a man to acknowledge that there is a better way of action or that his concepts have been mistaken is a major crisis. That's why true conversion is a literal turning around and is difficult. It's why so many persons retreat into the cliche, "You can't teach an old dog new tricks."

The problems of integration or the redistricting of a school boundary can create emotional explosions and shocking action justifying the comment, "A population undergoing change is a population of misfits, and misfits live and breathe in an atmosphere of passion."

It must have been this difficulty which confronted Jesus as he talked quietly about changed points of interpretation concerning the Commandments. "You have heard it said of old time," he said, and then confronted his listeners with the new saying, "But I say unto you."

This jolt from the old complacency into a new and changed conscience-searing experience was too great for these men. They reacted in anger, causing the frequent structured references to attempts to throw rocks at him, or to run him out or town, or to have him tried as a traitor. We read these facts of history and wonder. Yet go to a neighborhood confronting this same injunction, "There was an old way - but now there is a new way," and one confronts the same verbal backbites, emotional threats and desire to expel the irritant.

Basic in our faith is not only the knowledge that we can have the inner security to confront change but also the guidance of God to move calmly through change.

Said Jesus, "In this world you will have tribulation. But be of good cheer, I have overcome the world." Here's a faith that is certain of change and equally as certain of the underground faith to meet it with a singing spirit.

Paradoxes of Our Own Making

Robert Browning once said that paradoxes comfort while they mock. We live in a time which illustrates the situation in every day's events.

There was a time when the paradox existed in the fact that the people of the Christian faith could be described as "sorrowful yet always rejoicing, as poor yet making many riches, as having nothing yet possessing all things." We have the reversal of this in our situation.

Our paradox is that we have the finest media communication in history and yet we have difficulty in communicating with groups within our own cities. The launching of an astronaut can be viewed by millions; news can be telecast and literally bounced by Telstar to the nations of the earth.

At this very moment cultural groups may find it difficult to speak with one another in their own neighborhoods. Families may discover that it is impossible to speak to fellow-members in their own household. The technical advance comforts; the lack of understanding mocks.

A parallel paradox resides in our exploration of space while we permit an ignorance of our own inner selves. Think of the wealth of idealism in this country as illustrated by sacrificial missionaries and adventurous Peace Corpsmen.

Yet at this very moment we have been unable to understand our own selves. So hundreds of missionaries discover their work hampered because a few churches closed their doors to their fellow men in our own country.

We are looking farther into space and missing our own selves. And when we go to the moon we shall have to take our own selves!

We are comforted by our ability to reach out; we are mocked by our inability to reach in.

Walk around your own hometown and you may be shocked at the ugliness to which you've become accustomed and which you would not like a tourist from Europe to see.

We are comforted by the knowledge that we can protect our cities; we are mocked by our ignoring of that which we protect. The list of paradoxes grows. The problems of freedom and conformism, the challenge of leisure, our liberty from backbreaking toil and our boredom, our credulousness of every kind of will-o'-the-wisp and our lack of faith - these and others taunt us.

We have many self-contradictions. Yet there is still the reversal of our agony.

We can share love as easily as hate; we can inspire as quickly as we discourage; we can communicate truth as readily as falsehood; we can be held by the very power of God which we cannot understand. We are comforted by the presence of God, a presence that haunts us. That is our paradox.

Human Drama: God's In It Too

A recent trip to Stratford in Ontario underscores the enduring miracle of Shakespeare. In a time when the problems of the aging constitute political and social controversy and the dealing with suffering adds new accents to an ancient question, the tragedy of Lear speaks with relevance. After 400 years this play, with its Gothic proportions, provides the area for discussion, dramatizing the ancient and ever-present problem. The characters are boldly etched, unrelentingly marching toward their destiny with only Lear finding a transforming and redeeming quality.

In our own time such artists as the late Albert Camus, or the Korean author Kim, or the motion picture producer Bergman restate these themes. Most of us find them harsh; for we have been accustomed to the happy ending.

Somehow, the hero of the Western drama needs to ride triumphant into the sunset while the villain languishes in exile and in jail. Yet every day renews the tragedy.

A man gives his life in a great idealism and loses his life. A citizen, filled with talent and ability, becomes his own worst enemy and stands in his own light. Generations stand opposed to each other, each unwilling to understand or communicate.

So the tragedies of jealousy, ambition, ingratitude and prejudice are spun out. This string is "of imagination all compact."

We need to take these long, hard looks at life. There are enormous problems of life and death, illness and health, happiness and despair. Such questions we duck and dodge. All too often we leave them unanswered and find no faith to sustain us in the time of doubts.

We're like a gentle lady who once lived nearby. She found herself amazingly interested in the wrestling matches.

She'd watch this ridiculous fantasy, but sometimes it became too much for her gentle spirit. So she'd hold her hands in front of her face if it got to be too much. She didn't turn the set off. She didn't look when it got to be too rough.

There are too many of us who hide behind our own hands so that we miss the misery, the unanswered griefs, the tragedies of life. So we have no faith to sustain us in the testing moments. There is no way to forget.

This seems to be the time when "wisdom and goodness to the vile seem vile...Humanity must perforce prey on itself like monsters of the deep."

Thus the 250 and more characters of Shakespeare's dramas march across this stage and we find something of the counterpart in each day. He wrote, in his own way, the underscoring of an ancient moral truth, "Be not deceived; God is not mocked: for whatsoever a man soweth, that shall he also reap."

Even In the Shadows

In our part of the country, people talked about the groundhog seeing his shadow just a month ago. We wanted to be seeing the tips of tulips and daffodils by this time but there was that shadow to frighten off spring. It's just a legend, but then such things influence people. Perhaps a part of the cold wintry hatred of mankind is simply that we are frightened by our own shadows!

I have a little shadow
That goes in and out with me,
And what can be the use of him
Is more than I can see.

I join Robert Louis Stevenson in that comment.

The truth is that shadows have connoted fright. The lengthened shadow of Hitler fell across mankind. A British commentator said the other day that this year had begun under the shadow of the deaths of T. S. Eliot and Winston Churchill. It's the awareness that there is a fright in some shadows, either of the hatred that comes or the greatness that goes.

There's also the refreshment of the shadow. The shadow of a mighty rock in a weary land or the shadow of the valley where the heat wasn't quite as destroying has lured men through the ages. To those who have a profound sense of purpose in their lives there's the awareness of sustaining strength "even in the valley of the shadow of death."

Shadows are possible because of the bright light that shines. That's why institutions are really the lengthened shadows of those who live brilliantly. That's as true for the individual who feels of little consequence as it is for the world's great personalities. That's why it's a tragedy to hole up, pretending that there can be no spring.

I remember one of those pencil-thin teenagers who was described to me as being so slim that in his tight clothing he wouldn't even cast a shadow. Some of us live so thinly that there's no bulk or substance to our lives, no shadow to cast, and nothing to carry on the tradition and the high hopes.

Already there are the evidences of spring, even in the northlands. There's a difference in the shadows and maybe a new certitude of the meaning of our relationships.

There's a great prayer out of the distant shadows, that needs to be restated in our contemporary existence.

> O Lord. Support us all the day long until the shadows lengthen and the evening is come, and the busy world is hushed, and the fever of life is over, and our work is done. Then in thy mercy grant us a safe lodging and a holy rest, and peace at the last.

But until the shadow lengthen, let there be the awareness of sustaining guidance in the thick of things and the courage never to be frightened by our own shadow!

Overleaf: God So Loved the World

The tourist in Rome or Athens is impressed by the majestic columns, fragments of enormous buildings, which indicate a glory that has passed. One can imagine the Forum, the ancient theater or the many-columned temple.

This summer we found a little book in Rome which combined the present and the past. On one page the present ruins were portrayed while on the opposite page, printed on a plastic material, was the picture of the original. By placing the overleaf page on the picture of the present ruins, one could see how the remnants are the suggestion of the original glory.

It is this overleaf which is missing from so many of our situations. We look at the wreckage of a man, view the ruin of some dream of society or see some fellow with his reputation ruined, and we write it all off as failure. We dismiss the question of the Psalmist concerning mankind, "What is man that thou are mindful of him - Thou hast made him a little lower than the angels!"

What we need to see in the life of Christ is this overleaf, this awareness that man is meant to be more. Mankind is worth loving, worth dying for, and that's the overleaf which is put on the ruins as you look at a Cross.

On the campus of a nearby university there are some columns, the remnants of a building which once stood in our central city. No one knows what to do with them. No one has come up with the proper blueprint or the financial subsidy. So the ruins remain.

There are the similar ruins among ethnic, racial or cultural groups of the city where so many have failed to catch the dream of the blueprint or have failed to actually try to build the structure. So people are prejudged, and the blueprints are missing.

In the present discussions which go on in all of our countries, ranging from human freedom to housing, there's too much prejudging. The present fact is accepted rigidly as though nothing could ever be done about it. With this narrowed judgment, a man can go his way and see no need to try to do anything about the human situation. Wrote T. S. Eliot, noting this sense of guilt,

> It's not the feeling of anything I've ever done, which I might get away from, or anything in me I could get rid of - but of emptiness, or failure, towards someone, or something, outside myself; and I feel I must...atone - is that the word?"

That's the word and it puts the overleaf above the ruins we contrive. That's why these days demand that we seek in communication the fact that man is made in the image of God. God so loved the world - that's "overleaf'" enough to keep us working at the ruins - our own, as well as our neighbor's.

Fragility of Human Defenses

The meeting was announced, the speaker had been secured, and the plans had been completed. And then, two days before the event, the office building which was being erected next door caused a change of plans. The blasting for the foundations caused cracks to appear in the walls of Orchestra Hall in Chicago and so I had to speak in another building until the assurances could be given for the safety of the old hall. Everything in the old building had seemed to be satisfactory until they began to blast.

But that's the problem of these days. Everything seems to be all right with many of us and with many of our institutions until someone begins to blast. Then plans that other people make, the invasions on our time and schedules, the seemingly unrelated events suddenly cause cracks which one can resent but with which we have to deal. Sometimes the walls of our old bureaucratic structures are more vulnerable than we imagined. Will the structure last for another year?

Truman Douglas once commented:

> The disintegration of our society has revealed the fragility of just those things in which modern man has put his trust: material comfort, a relatively stable social structure, the right to live his own life undisturbed by events outside the circumference of his own freely chosen interest.... He is vulnerable to the invasions of God who makes himself known when our human securities are shaken.

It is the fragility of our defense that is so disturbing. We would like to think that there aren't any cracks, and that we're safe from any of the shocks of existence. Or, as Auden wrote: "The fears we know are of not knowing."

What to do? You can't prevent the blasting for buildings and just when we're safest there's the threat of trouble.

During the recent atrocities in the Congo I've heard men saying, "Why do we have our people over there?" Yet most of these men and women, missionaries, teachers, physicians and anthropologists have been working at peaceful pursuits. They had felt the tremors when no one else was aware, and they had responded with their own careers. Now they've paid with their lives. Now the shock waves reach our own little buildings.

It's apparent that we can't avoid or evade the shocks and we can't run from them. We can sink some new foundations for our own faith, re-examine the building of our own values, and rethink the meaning of life. Too many of us have been content to think of our safety in terms of the vulnerable building of our possessions. Once more the ancient words of Jesus come with clarity: "Every one who hears my words and does them will be like a wise man who built his house upon a rock; and the rains fell and the floods came, and the winds blew and beat upon that house but it did not fall because it was founded upon a rock!"

That's an important word at the end of a year and at the beginning.

Chapter IV. Forgive. Open Doors. Care.

- **From the first column in this section, Forgive to Restore:**
  Forgiveness comes in the midst of an experience, not in the dispensing of some impersonal charity.

- **From last column in this section, Free to Pray:**
  It's easier to be vociferous in our freedoms instead of understanding what it is we are free to do and free to be. We would rather be activists than thinkers. We would rather praise prayer than pray prayers.

Forgive To Restore

Among the most praised and least practiced of virtues is that of forgiveness. An amazing number of people who pray every day "Forgive us our trespasses" continue to bear ancient grudges, keeping the hurts as though they were members of the family. A little soul-searching can generally reveal that too many of us who espouse the worth of forgiveness miss the experience of actually overcoming an irritating hurt or healing a broken friendship. Too often we regard forgiveness as a sign of weakness instead of an adventure in strength.

Forgiveness is renewal. To forgive is to restore. Too much of our attitude about forgiveness is that it is the patronizingly superior ego which says "I forgive you" as though with quick fingers we were giving something to someone.

Forgiveness comes in the midst of an experience, not in the dispensing of some impersonal charity. It must be something of this spirit that inhabits those who value antiques. Refurbishing requires a knowledge of style, a recognition of integrity in wood or metal, an appreciation of original beauty. If that is understood, then layers of varnish and years of grime can be forgiven. But that forgiveness is not a published statement; it is a tedious working at the idea. It's the careful scrubbing of the piece of furniture, removing the old varnish, strengthening the weakened piece, and keeping at it until what someone else has called "junk" is now restored to classic beauty.

In Jesus' story of the Prodigal Son, he noted that the boy had run away from home and wasted the family inheritance. He had abused his body and torn up the old family traditions. In the end he was broke, hurt, trying to maintain existence and stave off starvation by working in the most menial of jobs.

He was junk. But to his father he is a son, and when he comes home there is a robe awaiting him and a welcoming into the family circle. That which others only saw as a delinquent boy, the father saw as a member of the household.

In our swift rush through life, we are too ready to tag labels on peoples or groups or races and remember some ancient violation of custom instead of some recognition of what we were meant to be. We even have trouble forgiving ourselves, nursing our own ancient sins instead of knowing the grace of forgiveness.

The Lord's Prayer places before men of all faiths a possibility of day-by-day understanding of the whole process of renewal. We pray God to forgive us as we forgive our brothers. We know God's forgiveness. It's a part of the contract that our brother know that also. Remembering the classic beauty of mutual understanding, seeing the possibility of personal growth, we can set about the tedious business of removing the layers of accrued hurts. What someone else called junk we see as renewed familyhood.

America doesn't know what to do with its junk. Its abandoned automobiles create an esthetic problem. Its larger problem is what to do with its junked community and human relations. There is the possibility of renewal, not of discard. To forgive is to restore. We need to work at that possibility.

When It's Not In The Book

A widely known man was stranded recently en route to a speaking engagement. His plane developed mechanical difficulties, and the airlines agent announced that passengers would proceed by bus. A few moments later, another airline announced a plane departure for the original destination.

One of the passengers hurriedly inquired concerning the possibility of departing on that plane. **"But," protested the agent, "there isn't a plane. It isn't listed in the book."** The agent admitted that he hadn't inquired at other passenger desks, simply because he saw no listing in the book.

The event is indicative of the world in which we live. Most of the situations we encounter aren't listed. Where do you find rules on how to behave at sit-ins or sit-downs, or in assertive protest against the violation of human rights? That is why creative and imaginative spirits which combine both restraint and boldness are required!

Perhaps you recall the speech of the late Gen. MacArthur at the signing of the treaty with Japan. There was no possible listing in the book even for that. One might have accepted the traditional and embarrassing humiliation of the conquered. Instead, the General approached the conquered with dignity, respected some of the ancient traditions and spoke of the problem confronting the world as a theological question instead of a political one.

Where would you find that listing in the book - unless you read the New Testament?

In similar fashion, the late Sen. Robert Taft, familiarly known as "Mr. Integrity," knew how to go beyond the listings in the book. During the Nurenberg trials he was concerned about the moral responsibilities of those judgments.

It was a time when he was prominently considered as the next Republican candidate for the presidency. It was an issue on which he might have been silent. Yet the blunt and honest senator from Ohio insisted that there was no justification for the trials, which violated the fundamental principles of American law that a man cannot be tried under the ex-post facto statute.

He was taunted by his enemies, pilloried by his competitors yet his was a voice that was raised at a needful time. In a time when responsible social action and imaginative understanding are required, none of us can settle for "playing it safe." Traditional structures may falter. Accustomed attitudes will have to be rethought.

Opening Doors

The crooner was singing "Just us in a room, without windows or doors." Frankly, that doesn't sound too inviting, suggesting a cell instead of a room. And there is the old limerick:

> I wish that my room had a floor,
> I don't mind it not having a door;
> But this walking around
> Without touching the ground
> Is getting to be quite a bore!

But I would be concerned if there was no door!

The challenge of this new year is discovering those doors. And then opening them.

Mankind is haunted by the number of bolted doors, areas where hope is abandoned. Think of the problems caused by totalitarian governments, or housing or racial injustice or extreme poverty and you are aware of the numbers of people who can't see a door.

What is worse, there are the others who know there are doors and refuse to open them. They can tell you all of the hazards, the disappointments and the risks.

- To be doorless in such a room is to be a victim of the heresy of despair. The doorless are hopeless.
- To pretend that there are doors that open to easy ways by which these problems can be solved is to live in a fantasy-land.
- To refuse to open the doors that are there is to be a defeatist and a cynic.

Men who collect such information tell us that doors have many meanings. There is the old tradition in certain rural areas of painting the door blue when there were marriageable daughters at home. There are the churches with red doors. There

68

were the doors to the castles with their great hinges of metal and their formidable look of authority. There are the glass doors that sometimes pose threats because they are confused with windows. The important fact to know is that there are doors. Personally, the most important significance of the door is the **open door**.

There is a sentence at the opening of a newly published book of essays by the late Pierre Teilhard de Chardin. That distinguished scholar and priest wrote, "The whole future of the earth, as of religion, seems to me to depend on the awakening of our faith in the future." That's an open door.

Think of the differences in persons and communities when there are those who understand the meaning of the Lord who says, "Behold, I stand at the door and knock. To any man who opens, I will come in and sup with him." At the opening of the year, open the door!

Movements, Not Monuments

Locked up - A friend of mine, who is a remarkably knowledgeable fellow, was sharing some of his reactions from world travels the other evening. Among his reflections was an interpretation of the magnificent temple of Karnak. The traveler commented on the piety and faith of these people who had built such an enormous tribute to their God.

To which his guide responded, "You have missed the point of all of this architecture. These people did not build the temple to pay tribute, but rather to enclose their god. They didn't want him wandering around, meddling with their affairs. So they built a tremendous temple to keep him in."

A heaviness upon heaviness - Something of the same symbolism carries over into the construction of the pyramids. Built as tombs for royalty, they became the masterful memorials not only to kings but to a literal "heaviness upon heaviness." That is, they became the tombs for power, a way to hold a tremendous idea.

Is this what we want to do with religion? Do we want to entomb it? Or enshrine it? And keep the idea from moving in our midst?

Modern attempts to entomb - Most men would immediately deny that this is desirable. Yet our very acts often collide with our words.

For instance recently a Jewish rabbi in Alexandria, Va., spoke out against segregation even though the mayor of the city is a member of his congregation. Personal friendships and membership in the synagogue were at stake. Should he have kept quiet? Should he keep God in the temple?

Or a Roman Catholic bishop spoke out in New Orleans on the same subject. Not all of his members agree with the bishop and there have been groups protesting his acts. At stake is the membership of the people in their church. Should he have kept God inside the church?

Or here is a recent assembly of a group of members of the National Council of Churches of Christ in America. In their discussion they suggested that the foreign policy of the United States concerning Red China ought to be reviewed. Immediately there were men who suggested withdrawing support from the Council. What business is it of the churches? Keep God out of international affairs? Keep God in the temple?

Even when we disagree - Fortunately, there are enough men and women in our society aware of the need of an active conscience, concerned lest the name of God became associated with tranquilizers instead of prophetic righteousness. There are alert businessmen who are supporting their churches even when they personally cannot agree with its pronouncements.

Pulpit and pew together - All of this constitutes a serious problem and challenge. The ministry of religion is not to support other people who speak for a fact personally unacceptable. We are not righteous when we subsidize that which we would not imitate.

Nonetheless, it is this witness which is like an alarm bell, signalling the community to something which is wrong and needs concerned action. At least, to such people, God is not locked up some place.

Movements, not monuments - In Washington, D.C., there used to be a church (maybe it's still there) with the words inscribed over its doorway, "A Monument to God." I wanted to climb up and chisel the words off of that stone. God needs no monuments; He does desire movements.

The history of the world has put the lie to every attempt to lock God in any temple of Karnak, pyramid in Egypt or any other structure. **What a man believes matters down to the very last detail of his life. His faith matters when he gets it out of the tombs.**

71

To Love Enough - Which is to Care Enough

"God never asks the impossible. He does ask us to do what we can, and then to ask for what we cannot do." The words are St. Augustine's. The concept is necessary for today.

Our predicament is we're too likely to decide we can't achieve some goal and so we settle for nothingness. To pray for that which we can't achieve on our own is a requisite of a great conviction of faith. To fail to ask is to fade into our environment with no yearning for the change.

In a sense, the basic need is that somebody cares. Saroyan said that you have to care even to play baseball. Caring enough is an ingredient for any act. Only those who care enough do what they can, or have the boldness to pray for that which they can't do.

Only those who care enough will have the imagination to pray the right prayer and to hear the right answer.

William Stringfellow, the Christian attorney whose writings have disturbed some consciences, tells of the day he was hurrying for a plane when a churchman called, asking legal advice for a person. The lady was going to be evicted.

Stringfellow urged the clergyman to sell some of the church tapestries, and so pay the rent. He hung up and hurried for the plane. It was a radical thing to suggest.

Insists Stringfellow:

> The tapestry hanging in the church becomes and is a wholesome and holy thing only if the congregation which has the tapestry is free to take it down and sell it in order to feed the hungry and care for the sick, or pay the rent, or in any other way serve the world. The

tapestry is authentically a Christian symbol only when it represents freedom in Christ.

That's enough to startle your conscience when you ask, "But what can I do about it?" Most of us haven't canvassed all of the possibilities of what we can do about all the moral and social issues which demand action. We just haven't decided how much we're ready to give up - or, for that matter - how much we're ready to take on. To pray for that which we can't achieve demands that we come to some new commitments of purpose.

To really know love is to realistically care. It isn't giving a bit of service to some cause which can list your name as a sponsor. To love enough - which is to care enough - is to bring a person or an institution to that point where what might have been a sacrifice becomes a natural act.

We aren't asked to do the impossible. We are asked to expect the impossible. Our impossibles are still God's possibles. That's why we pray, "Thy kingdom come, Thy will be done."

Free To Pray

What is the heritage of this nation? Shall we be known for our energy, our inventive genius, our material resources, our blending of the cultures of the earth, our guarantee of responsible freedoms, or our luxuries? The list is long. What is important, our real heritage, needs to be renewed in every generation.

For instance, a cartoon during this past week illustrated the problem. The artist portrayed four golfers out on the links on a Sunday morning. The church bell was ringing in the nearby steeple. The one golfer was telling the other, "Those Supreme Court justices ought to be fired for telling us that we can't pray in our schools."

It's easier to be vociferous in our freedoms instead of understanding what it is we are free to do and free to be. We would rather be activists than thinkers. We would rather praise prayer than pray prayers.

I remember visiting an elderly man in a hospital ward. After I had prayed with this patient, the man in the next bed asked me to pray with him. I suggested that he pray first, and then I would lift a prayer for him.

"Oh," he said, "I don't know a prayer."

"But I'm sure that you do," I said, "for prayer is conversation with God. Just talk in your own way."

Then he smiled and I listened as this gaunt wizened man of 92 years prayed, "Now I lay me down to sleep."

It was pathetically beautiful and poignantly sad. He was praying the prayer of his childhood. It was a good prayer. But he had missed the whole lifetime adventure of prayer. Would he have been one of those who was shocked to have prayer banned

74

from the schoolroom when he had banned it from his own life? This may be our crisis.

When Thomas Wolfe probed the spirit of this country 20 years ago, he wrote, "I believe that we are lost here in America, but I believe that we shall be found.. .I think that the true fulfillment of our spirit, of our people, of our mighty and immortal land, is yet to come."

All of us who believe in the heritage and spirit of this country believe this. All of us who love this country will want to hope and work for this. Some of us will pray for it.

Chapter V. Choices... Goodness and mercy follow those who serve the Lord

- **From the first column in this section, A Time For Constraint:**
  Constraint is an inner discipline. Think of the causes in any city that would be blessed if some people would use inner constraint instead of blasting with unrestrained invective.

- **From the last column in this section, Choices and Destiny:**
  Since we must choose and even silence is decision - there are qualities that can be noted about our choices.... Choices limit the field... Choices determine destiny.

A Time for Constraint

A few days ago Dr. Saul Alinsky commented that all too many people in northern cities want to keep things quiet. He called it a "zoo mentality," an attempt to keep people caged, quiet, and, if not complacent, at least silent. He's right about it.

There are, undoubtedly, structures in every city that want to keep life free from controversy. As Ralph Sockman once said, "There are people who, if they saw the Lord coming down one side of the street and the devil coming down the other, would say, 'Here, you two ought to get together.' "

This is the problem of restraint. Men can be restrained by tyrants, by laws, or by their own habits. But they can also be restrained by their own inability to speak. If a man is in danger of economic or social jeopardy, he can be easily restrained. On the other hand there are good restraints. The traffic law which encourages a driver to handle the power of his automobile in a careful manner is a good restraint. I may be driving within legal limits, yet if I see a motorcycle policeman following me, I look at my speedometer and I feel the definite sense of restraint.

There is also the restraint that comes from fear. The President doesn't use nuclear power or bomb certain cities or escalate the war in certain ways because he must act in a restrained way. The possibilities of nuclear destruction are too awful to contemplate.

There's another word that needs to be explored in these days, namely the fine concept of constraint. There's no zoo mentality about that. **Constraint is an inner discipline. Think of the causes in any city that would be blessed if some people would use inner constraint instead of blasting with unrestrained invective.**

Constraint doesn't lash out in unrestrained language. It doesn't bluster or threaten nor does it lie down in shameful apathy. Constraint has the quality of moral responsibility. You can be restrained by law but constrained by love.

The problem of too many people is that they are restrained by their own fears. They're afraid to do what they know they ought to do. As John Ciardi once said, "In this security-conscious society of ours we're so afraid of going broke that we're afraid to go for broke."

There are too many people in our segregated clubs and civic groups who are restrained by their own fears. They're afraid of what someone will say. There are too many people in a neighborhood who are afraid to speak with courage. They're afraid of what someone will say.

It's easy enough to slash out with abrasive words or irresponsible acts. What so many citizens need to explore is the ancient statement, "For the love of Christ constraineth us." J.B. Phillips translates that, "The very spring of our actions is the love of Christ."

There are social injustices to be dealt with in our time. There are areas which have the need of communication. There are honest people who have been working and are continuing to work to meet these needs, secure this justice and build a community in which every man is free, uncaged from either another man's tyranny or his own restraints. It is a time for constraint, a time when "the love of Christ allows us no choice."

You, Too, Are Responsible

"Who's responsible here?" That question, asked by a policeman at the height of a neighborhood disturbance, can be repeated in any number of situations. Look at the bumper-to-bumper traffic of many of our highways and you can ask, "Who's responsible here?"

Examine the acres of below par housing and slums and then ask, "Who's responsible here?"

When a parent admits that he has seen little of his teenage children and tells a teacher that "the school sees more of my child than I do," the question can be asked, "Who's responsible here?"

One of the difficult explorations for mankind is this understanding of responsibility. Dr. H. Richard Niebuhr believed that the idea was of very recent origin as a symbol of our acts. Ancient words such as duty, virtue, goodness, and morality were common: but "responsibility" was a newer word. Yet the search for responsibility has been an experience as old as mankind. "Am I my brother's keeper?" was Cain's question.

As civilization began to express itself, man was constantly confronting the fact that while a few might be guilty, all could be responsible.

If there is a community breakdown or a loss of morale, you must ask the groups of that community what they have done to establish morale. You won't ask the federal government. Basic to the development of this sense of responsibility is a new understanding of our involvement in communities, because we have developed a personal relationship to eternal values. Personal responsibility is the extension of the self not only to one's fellow, but also to values which give meanings to all persons. That's why the ancients spoke of responsibility in these terms:

"We ought so to fear and to love God" so as to do certain things. Our honesty, integrity, relationship to our fellows is dependent upon this initial responsibility to God. A man loves God; therefore he doesn't lie or steal.

Suppose someone from outside this planet came into the midst of many of the national and international tensions and asked the question, "Who's responsible here?"

It is the conviction of a mature faith that while some are guilty, all are responsible. It is to this quality of extraordinary responsibility in the ordinary events of today that man expresses his response in grateful vocation.

Much Depends on Little

It's fascinating to see how dominating ideas are often built on the tiniest of experiences. We know that small events can determine large issues. The old business of "for want of a nail that battle is lost" is really a fact. Woodrow Wilson is reputed to have felt that the Versailles Treaty was influenced in part by the fact that his too-tight shoes hurt his feet. By that tiny experience some of the destiny of nations hung.

Likewise, scraps of experience can determine the opinions or attitudes of whole generations. One small experience is magnified out of proportion and the battle for truth or honor is lost.

The scientist may be able to construct an image of the dinosaur from a very few bones. If he has some mental picture of the dinosaur and is able to make an educated guess from the bones at his disposal, he may come up with a reasonably accurate description.

Yet his guess requires discipline, demands a sense of history, depends upon a patient expression of logic and insists upon a perspective of the whole.

Look at the unscientific way in which we take up one of those bones in human relations. The other week I was visiting in a hospital and met a man who had been irritated by a happening in a church in 1903.

He was unhappy because a boys' choir had been eliminated in favor of another form of choir. On that experience he pulled out. What's more, he constructed a dinosaur out of the bone. He thought about it, nursed it, watched it grow and, 60 years later in a hospital, he is possessed by it. When I asked him about his church relations, he recounted that ancient story as though is had happened yesterday. Only one scrap of experience and he had allowed a dinosaur of a grudge to embitter his life.

One might write that off as the eccentric experience of an odd personage. Yet an analysis of the tensions between nations and races and groups is often as illogical. On a few scraps of experience, we construct the wrong dinosaur.

Once upon a time this might be regarded as the foolishness of the family feud or the dispute of the clan. Now the enormity of power that is vested in our nations makes this problem critical. The same essentials demanded of the scientist are demanded of each of us.

Only those who are creatively able to examine their scraps of experience in the light of yesterday's truth and today's needs are able to patiently strive for the healing of the world.

So you've had an experience - a small but significant one. Before you construct your dinosaur from that one bone, take a long, patient and logical look.

Generalities Cover Up

Generally speaking, generalities are inaccurate. Or almost always, as the Gilbert and Sullivan lyrics would add. Yet generalities are indulged in so frequently that they hamper solution of many demanding social problems.

During one evening recently two television panel discussions discussed problems confronting young people. One group insisted that cheating was prevalent because of parents who demanded grades at any cost. Another panel on another channel insisted as vigorously that juvenile delinquency was on the rise because all parents had lost a sense of responsible concern. Such generalities are too easy, too pat, to solve problems.

- Think of the times when all Protestants, or all Catholics, or all Jews have been put into a single box and labeled.
- If there is a rise in crime, are all policemen at fault?
- If there is moral crisis, are all clergymen inept?
- If the Russians loft a satellite, are all American educational systems inferior?

Any family can have a soul-searching experience analyzing its own table talk, discovering that too-frequent tolerance of the easy generalization.

Our lives are based upon some generalizations which have be come a foundation. The concept that all men are the children of God and capable of understanding the love of God is basic. Our Constitution is filled with them, which is why critics conclude that these are "glittering generalities" when they find their own generalities challenged.

When Jesus told the story of the Good Samaritan, he deliberately walked into such an area. To speak of Samaritans and Jews is a generalization. But one man stops to help another man along the way, and suddenly something in the old, hateful wall is breached.

From this vantage point men can see each other in terms of what they really are, instead of in an irrational generalization.

Just as mature persons grow beyond shallow gossip and hurtful slander, so this same maturity brings a person beyond the easy generalization and the dogmatizing of surface opinions. Some social situations seem to be beyond personal control, but we are all responsible at this point. Or almost all!

On The Beam

From time to time it has been my privilege to fly in military aircraft while en route to speaking engagements of the Air Force. I've stood in the cock pit, watching a pilot "lock the plane in," setting it on an automatic device. The beam from the outside became the guide for the plane. It became standard for the trip. But what happens if someone tampers with the standard, or deflects the beam?

A few years ago a three-panel cartoon showed a person scowling while looking at the marker on the scales. So this person got off, adjusted the lever, and then smiled as the lever registered 10 pounds lighter. That's an easy way to lose weight. But what happens to our standards of weights and measures when we tamper with the lever?

This is why we have to be concerned in these days of permissive morality.

The noteworthy Bishop of Woolwich wrote recently, "My concern is that Christians, in love as in war, should have the terrible freedom with which God has endowed us, and should exercise it responsibly. They must decide for themselves, though this certainly does not mean that they must decide on their own."

This is what the "hate groups" in our country seem to miss. They proclaim a concern for our nation. They are for patriotism which they interpret as nationalism. They're for pride of heritage which they interpret as some ethnic superiority. We all have to make decisions in these matters, but these decisions have to be in terms of the wholes and not in fragments, in terms of eternal values and not in terms of passing fancies.

It is the faith of the Christian that he is a free person, but he is not here on his own. His values have to be larger than just to win. He knows that he can tune in to that beam. He knows that he can understand the weights and measures. So patriotism is not nationalism. Loving one's country does not mean that one has to hate one's neighbor. Pride of heritage is not idolatry of ancestry. Loving one's grandparents does not mean that one has to ignore another person's ancestry.

We have been accustomed to thinking that we could lock our plane in and somehow muddle through. This self-infatuation can only result in a kind of tampering with the beam. We may think that we can win votes by adjusting the scales. That's been tried before and it has worked - temporarily. Hitler got away with it. Mussolini got away with it. Others will try.

In the end there is the terrible freedom to decide for ourselves, but not on our own. So St. Paul counseled, "Let love be genuine; hate what is evil, hold fast to that which is good; love one another with brotherly love; outdo one another in showing honor." That's keeping on the beam. That's weighing on the proper scales.

Don't Give Me Talk; Show Me!

It's one thing to hold a certain moral principle; it's another thing to tell your neighbor about it. For instance, to believe in excellence in education is one thing; to share that faith with a neighbor is another thing. Is it necessary to do it? To believe in integrity in political government is one thing; to discuss the matter with a neighbor in order to bring him to a point of view is another. The debates have been vigorous.

Yet some of the persons who have defended the right of the individual not to discuss his moral principles, watched the expulsion of students because they had violated honor codes and had cheated. The issue of whether a man should go along with his fellows, or report the violation of the code is another example of the same problem. Should you just win by cheating? What are the demands of the code of honor?

Before you answer that question, take a long look at what is happening in many areas of our country. To wink at injustice or to keep quiet when a wrong is tolerated creates an erosion in agreed upon values. When that coherence goes, then mankind confronts a serious problem.

Peter Marshall once prayed, "O Lord, help us to stand for some thing lest we fall for anything." That eminent Scottish theologian, John Baillie, prayed, "Forgive us, Lord, the unkind word and the unkind silence." It's the unkind silence that creates the bland, meaningless apathy that tolerates evil, winks at injustice, and concludes that there's nothing that anyone can do about it. Someone has to stand against the wrong or the unkind silence condemns us.

There is a fine incident that comes out of the Revolutionary War in American history. A Lutheran preacher by the name of Muhlenberg was also a colonel in the fledgling army.

One day he walked into his pulpit, wearing his preacher's robe. At the close of the sermon he is reported to have said, "There's a time to pray and a time to fight and this is the time to fight." Where upon he threw off his black gown, revealing his army uniform, and led the men of the congregation out to the tough task confronting them. It was one thing for him to hold a moral principle; it was another thing to share it with his neighbor. This is a contemporary fact to be considered as we confront the ancient discipline of Lent.

If you believe in racial justice, do you share that belief with your neighbor? Do you keep it to yourself?

Or could this be the time when we demonstrate in word and deed, the insistence of the song in *My Fair Lady*: "Don't talk of love, show me!"

Choices: Hinges of Our Destiny

This is a time of decision. There are numbers of confused people these days who insist that they'd like to run away, take a cruise, or hibernate. There are others who join the cries of the storm-beset sailors of Shakespeare's *The Tempest*: "All's lost. To prayers, to prayers."

Yet decisions must be made and, as Edwin Markham once insisted: "Choices are the hinges of destiny." Since we must choose - and even silence is decision - there are qualities that can be noted about our choices.

Choices limit the field. An artist uses one style and discards others. He limits the field but he still expresses a point of view. A musician develops a certain harmonic pattern and limits the field. John chooses Mary and limits the field. The voter casts a ballot and limits the field. These are the self-imposed limitations which choices make for our lives. So Scripture states: "Choose you this day whom you will serve. No man can serve two masters." Those are the deliberate moral choices which give us the paradox of limiting the field in order to have unlimited horizons!

Choices determine destiny. Napoleon fought on two fronts; Lee chose to serve the South; Lincoln chose to preserve the Union at all costs; Wilson decided to be true to his dream - these are typical historic moments which created life patterns for millions of people. The margin of one vote has been the difference between presidencies, or Supreme Court decisions, or important legislative acts. The choices men make individually and collectively become the determining factor not only for present but for the next generations as well. It is still true that the sins of the fathers are visited on succeeding generations and goodness and mercy follow those who serve the Lord.

Choices determined. Most of us feel caught in the beartrap of circumstances, with causes far too great for personal decision. Men are caught with limitations of health, nature, and enormous events.

Yet within these limitations we are still free to choose. Harry Emerson Fosdick once told of a woman who had suffered greatly, to whom he said: "My, but suffering does color your life."

"Yes," she replied, "but I choose the colors."

It's no wonder then that we have no right to be hiding behind some false piety or plea of busyness or lack of knowledge in the business of making these important decisions. What right have we to be handling out tranquilizers and hiding from contact with the tough issues of life, when important choices have to be made in this demanding world?

The ultimate choices are before us constantly. In a real sense, we're always in the voting booth. Either we serve God or mammon. Either we are pawns of events or servants of the Almighty. Either we fall for anything or stand for truth. Important decisions are to be made and once more "choices become the hinges of our destiny."

Chapter VI. The Whole World In His Hands

- **From the first column in this section, Remember This, America:**
  Kneel in prayer, America
  And know that
  God is not American

- **From last column in this section, The Fourth of July, 1967**
  We pray that...
  We may continue the courage to love mercy, to do justly and to walk humbly with our God.

Remember This, America!

Remember This, America!
Life should be peopled with memories
That strengthen, inspire, challenge.
Such memories are ours, America.
Here in this land, bounded by great oceans,
We had an image as great as our nation.
Here the centuries labored in the patient stillness of forest and
plain,
Here tons of water weighted this land
Until a wealth inherited, longed to be found.

Remember This, America!
Life should be blessed with a heritage
That makes the blood run faster
And the spirit swell with pride.
Here marched heroes who valued freedom more than safety,
Honor more than gain.
Here is the cradle which could hold this growing mass
Blended of the hopes of mankind.

Remember This, America!
Life should be blessed with singing spirits,
Walt Whitman singing, "O resistless, restless, race,.. Pioneers O
pioneers."
These are its songs,
telling its wondrous story:
Paul Revere's ride and Barbara Frietchie,
America the Beautiful and Columbia the Gem of the Ocean,
These and a thousand others,

The swelling tide of a land that could sing
Because it had something to sing about.
Singing with open mouths their strong melodious songs.

Remember This, America!
Life should have humble reverence,
That honest humility that comes not from groveling in slavery
But standing at full height
And seeing greatness stretching on beyond;
Such reverence that recognizes truth;
The humility that understands the vastness of
unexplored knowledge;
The wisdom that comes to those who know their
limitations.

Remember This, America!
Life should have a great faith.
This is God's world, not ours.
God's mountains they are with purpl'd majesty,
God's fruited plains, God's Niagara,
God's spirit working through the flesh of human beings,
Always bring familyhood through our broken ties.
Dig deep into this spirit, America.
This is no time to diminish our image before the world,
Kneel in prayer, America,
And know that
God is not American.
We believe that He has been doing great things through
America,
And would do greater things using Americans.
But He is not ours.
We are His.
Remember This, America!

Bridges to Understanding

Bridges are beautiful. The architects and engineers of such structures have been able to blend strength with beauty, merging endurance with grace. The Verazanno Bridge in New York and the Golden Gate Bridge in San Francisco are notable symbols of artistry.

Smaller bridges are also delightful. A little swinging bridge in picturesque Bettwsy-Coed in Wales caught our fancy. The quaint and fast-disappearing wooden-covered bridges in parts of our own country bring nostalgic memories.

Of all of the small bridges, none are more interesting than those tiny, orange-red ones in Japan. Hayakawa, the world-famous semanticist, says that these bridges are symbols of "small talk." When two friends meet, they discuss the weather, their health, or some other common interest in which no real information is circulated. It's important small talk. It's a little bridge, enabling two people to meet.

Our problem is that in all too many instances we're content to leave it that way. Fellowship becomes mere small talk, when honest community requires that we take neighborliness out of the slogan-stage. We need to meet on the bridge and then learn to span the differences.

Real fellowship occurs when persons of differing points of view traverse the bridge that stretches from their opposing cliffs and precipices, permitting them to discover a new sense of being bound together. There is commitment and understanding.

In all too many of our cities and communities there are groups which have no Verazanno bridge, no swinging bridge, not even a tiny Japanese bridge to cross the gaps of misunderstanding. When the bridges are down, communication is broken. Then, only a fuse is required to set off the explosive and irrational behavior which destroys so many hopes.

Thoreau once said that youth wants to build a bridge to the moon while the middle-aged are content to settle for a woodshed. Is the person who wants to reach across the gaps of ethnic, racial, cultural or religious groups just a dreamer? Do we have to settle for shacks when there is a possibility of building structures for the meeting of minds?

Who can count the number of riots and disturbances that might have been prevented had someone been willing to build a bridge and then travel it, discovering commitment and understanding...like bridges, especially the ones that are able to become the meeting places for those who bring their strength as well as their problems, their hopes as well as their hurts, their desires as well as their anger.

Those who build the bridges - sometimes those little bridges that span the small ditches of difference - make it possible for men to think and work together.

We Need the Right Glue

Among the humble and yet essential household items is that necessary item of glue. Once a smelly, sticky substance, it has become glamorized and attractively packaged. It's still glue. Necessary for repairs and mending, it is required in every household. What is also important is that the right substance is used as the cohesive agent.

Move out of the household into the larger areas of life and see how the wrong glue is used.

Critics insist that there are churches which are held together by social custom or ethnic factors. They are said to have become exclusive clubs instead of inclusive fellowships. If there are churches that are held together by people desiring social advantage, political prestige or economic preference, then the wrong glue is being used.

On almost every national occasion there are speakers who seem to equate democracy with religious convictions. Obviously, the presence of a great faith is going to feed the ideals of a nation. The very necessities of human dignity and responsible freedom require the essential of a religious conviction. But the use of religion as a kind of glue to hold the nation together is the wrong use of religious faith.

There are enough tensions and strains in life today. Men and women have breakdowns. Nations find old and trusted procedures shattered. The familiar maps are suddenly torn apart. Neighborhoods not only change, they break up. So do families.

Yet in the midst of such situations, there are other persons who stand firm and refuse to be shattered. There are neighborhoods that ride out of the storms unbroken. There are families that have withstood strains which have caused others to come apart.

St. Paul told the Corinthians that love could endure anything. "Love knows no limit to its endurance, no end to its trust, no fading of its hope; it can outlast anything." That's not a commercial for a religious glue; it's a description of a power which is quite different. Love is an interacting, uniting power. It changes and redeems. It doesn't just "glue together" a man and a woman. It brings them into the common, transcending and responsible relationship of husband and wife. It doesn't just glue together races; it brings them into an understanding familyhood.

We're held together by many cohesive relationships. Those persons and institutions that withstand the tensions have deep inner resources which hold them steady. It's important that we use the right kind of glue!

All in the Family of God

We were flying over a jungle in Malaya when a small storm jostled our tiny plane. My seatmate, a traveler from New Zealand, looking down at the swaying trees and the thick underbrush, shuddered and said, "If we came down here, not even God would know where we were." It wasn't a true statement, but we felt the loss.

A few weeks ago a Norwegian sailor died aboard a lake steamer. His family was abroad and so the funeral service was attended by no one but the pastor. It was a strange experience to stand alone, with no one there but the body of this not-so-old sailor. Yet there was a family in another port, and a letter could be written assuring that grieving family that the member of their family had received the rites of his faith. To them it must have seemed as though there was an immensity of loneliness, but one letter of understanding could break through.

Last week a little girl died in our city. She had been pursued by a whole series of unfortunate circumstances and had never known the happiness we associate with childhood. Now in her death, the clergyman who had been her friend was alone at this casket. No one had called to claim the body. No one had shed a tear. No one had done a thing to break through the immensity of loneliness.

It is the ironic fact in this crowded world that it is more and more impossible to be alone and more and more impossible to escape such loneliness. The immensity of the jungle is no more threatening than the jungle of the neighborhood where the young can die unnoticed and unmourned. The Norwegian sailor was kept in the friendship of his fellow-sailors and of his church. But the girl was not. This is our problem.

One man dying during the war was able to write:

> If I should die think only this of me:
> That there's some corner of a foreign field
> That is forever England.

But suppose he had not had the deep inbred loyalty with its remembrance of what he was. It is this that is more and more the poignant and the imposing challenge.

The ancient poet cried, "If I forget thee, let my right hand forget her cunning." We're always in the danger of forgetfulness, having the small plane of our existence jostled by some unseen sin and tempted to think that not even God would know, or could know, where we are.

In such a time of forgetfulness and nonsignificance, there is the thrust of the promise that all men are of the family of God. There is also the gnawing weight on our conscience that, knowing this, we make that known in a myriad ways so that none, in this polite or cruel jungle, shall ever think that they are forgotten.

Greatest Challenge - World In One Family

In these days when thoughtful people are concerned about the population explosion, some of us are concerned also about enlarging our families. Or put it this way: we need to discover the meaning of the larger family.

Good homes, like most other good things, can't be kept indoors. They are the slender but tough means by which much of life hangs together.

There is a Chinese proverb that puts it succinctly: "It is not enough that we be one world; we must be one family." This requires discipline and something more than wistful wishes. It demands not only the knowledge of the ideal but the will to do it.

It's a little like the son of Nels Ferre, a famous theologian. The youngster had been off for a few weeks in the summer, visiting indulgent relatives, where he enjoyed all of the luxuries and none of the responsibilities.

When he came home, his mother asked him to mow the lawn. His reply is classic: "Gee, I hate to do it, but I love to have to."

We grumble many times at the hours required for those disciplines which take our consciousness of our ties to one another out beyond our own households. Yet these are the uniting experiences which tie us into our larger familyhood. Someone may object that all of this is idealism. It certainly is.

But idealism of the finest kind is realism. Let a person try to put his ideals into practice and he'll find that out in a hurry.

The family becomes the laboratory, the proving ground and the experimental station where these ideals are put into practice and then developed in the world scene.

When Edward Weeks, the then editor of *The Atlantic Monthly*, visited London immediately after the war, he was impressed by the rebuilding that was going on. Most of all he noted the slender scaffolding surrounding the buildings upon which the craftsmen were working to recreate the ancient and famous city.

It is upon similar scaffolding - the slender ties of concern expressed in an infinite number of ways - that breaks between races, between divisions of society and hatreds between peoples are overcome.

Jesus looked about him asking, "Who is my mother and my brothers? Whoever does the will of God is my brother and sister and mother."

Of such is the larger family. The greatest experiment confronting mankind today is the willingness to use the solid rule of accumulated ethical understanding and get loose from the old.

The greatest experiment awaiting mankind today is the development of a willingness to push this sense of the enlarged family relationships into the practical disciplines of human relations.

We, the people, must become responsible members of the family...people who love to have to do it.

The Small Bridge, First

For more than 16 years, thousands of visitors to the United States and Canada from almost every country of the world have been the recipients of warm and sincere hospitality. Under the auspices of various organizations, such as World Hospitality, these visitors not only saw buildings, wonders of nature and factories. They spent weekends with new friends, explored kitchens and back yards, helped broil a steak or shared a family conversation.

Valuable as is this hospitality, no one supposes that it can solve international tensions. Life isn't quite that simple. Yet over and over again it has provided the bridge of friendship.

Why can't we try the same thing more frequently in our own neighborhoods? The subtleties of so many tensions in our cities, towns and villages demand that we break down the rigid barriers instead of perpetuating the "foreignness" of so many of our citizens.

Imagine what would happen if attorneys, ministers, carpenters, auto workers or housekeepers would entertain their parallel in some other racial or ethnic group. That wouldn't solve all of the problems but it would provide an area of understanding.

Hayakawa, the internationally famous semantics expert, has told of the value of "small talk." Two people can chat for a few minutes concerning the weather or sports or any other subject, simply learning to know one another. It is like the small bridges which the Japanese build across a ditch. They could step across, but the colorful little bridge provides the situation where two persons can meet and talk.

These small bridges of communication are needed in our communities. It is somewhat shocking to know how many of us have never had a speaking acquaintance or personal friendship with someone in a different ethnic, cultural, racial or educational pattern. We are so busy entertaining our friends that we become strangers to those who are outside our little circles.

The problems of the world are far too complex for any of us to solve by ourselves. Chatting in your own backyard with a man of a different accent or skin tone or cultural background won't solve them all, either. But it will build that small bridge.

It's something that any one of us can do now. It might be exciting to see what would happen if that movement spread across this hemisphere!

The Fourth of July 1967

This is the irony of our time:
We know how to communicate,
Having radio, television, even Telstar;
With public relations experts,
Skillful artisans at making our name as glittering
As that sparking geodesic dome.
And yet, in all too many places of this world,
We seem to fail and so must know,
America is not loved!

This is the frustration of our time:
For we want to be loved
We are those who like to be liked.
It has been our joy to meet
So many of the world's people who visit us,
And we have eagerly, even naively, asked:
"How do you like us?"
It puzzles and now gnaws at us that
America is feared!

This is the challenge of our time:
The ancient dream of a free people
Is threatened by a multitude
Of events, all confused and complicated.
Yet we remember George Washington insisting
That there is a "Union between virtue and happiness."
We would not be a power-mad people,
We would be humble, not arrogant, knowing that
America is still an unimagined promise!

This is the hope of our time:
That we renew the dream,
Possessing the nerve not to fail
At keeping the resolve to serve meekness
Before we stumble with a boastful anger.
Once more we now resolve not to "meanly lose
This last best hope of earth,"
To be in our integrity as well as in our fabled land
America the Beautiful!

This is the prayer of our time:
To know that higher patriotism -
"To live for principles as bravely as we fight for them.
We pray that in this revolutionary time
We may continue the courage to love mercy,
To do justly, and to walk humbly with our God.
Then shall others see in us that for which we strive -
America, a blessing for all mankind!

About Ralph Loew

Dale Anderson, News Staff Reporter for *The Buffalo News*, wrote the following obituary, included here as both an introduction and an indication of Loew's involvement with community issues:

The Rev. Ralph W. Loew, 88, pastor emeritus of Holy Trinity Lutheran Church and the dean of Buffalo clergymen, died Tuesday (March 5, 1996) in Sarasota, Fla., after suffering a heart attack while swimming in a pool.

Dr. Loew, a leader in the community's civic and religious life for half a century, was pastor of Holy Trinity from 1944 to 1975, and served for 10 years as the director of the Department of Religion at Chautauqua Institution.

He was the author of six books and for many years wrote a column, "From My Window," for the *Buffalo Courier-Express*. From 1960 to 1967, he also wrote a nationally syndicated weekly column, "Finding the Way."

His sermon "The Eternity of a Little While" was selected by *Life* magazine as one of the six notable Easter sermons of 1957.

As pastor of Holy Trinity, he resisted the trend toward suburbanization and encouraged the congregation's dedication to the city as the only Lutheran church in downtown Buffalo.

He oversaw the church's construction of a senior citizens' apartment building on Linwood Avenue behind church property on Main Street.

He worked closely with other churches in Holy Trinity's predominantly African-American neighborhood and was a pioneer in ecumenical endeavors with local Catholic churches. He was one of the organizers of Buffalo Area Metropolitan Ministries, the area's primary ecumenical group.

He declined offers to leave Holy Trinity for other positions in the 1960s, turning down the presidency of the new Upstate New York Synod of the Lutheran Church in America and the leadership of a multimillion-dollar Lutheran project in Chicago's Loop.

He served as president of the Community Action Organization and was a leader in campaigning for open housing in Buffalo. He also was coordinator of Project Good Neighbor.

He was president of the Ministerial Association, the Buffalo and Erie County Council of Churches, and the Governor's Youth Commission. He also was chairman of the Graduate School of Religious Studies at Canisius College.

He was also a member of the boards of directors of the former Deaconess Hospital and the Council on World Affairs and was a founder of Habitat/Buffalo, an affiliate of Habitat for Humanity. Gov. Nelson A. Rockefeller appointed him to the Empire State Foundation.

He encouraged a parishioner, Margaret L. Wendt, to establish the philanthropic foundation that bears her name and served for many years as one of the foundation's three trustees.

The Wendt Foundation has supported numerous projects in the area, including the restoration of Elbert Hubbard's Roycroft Inn in East Aurora..

Dr. Loew was the recipient of numerous awards. In 1966 he became the first clergyman to be honored by the Greater Buffalo Advertising Club as its Man of the Year. Last June, he was one of the first recipients of the inter-faith awards given by the Buffalo-Niagara Chapter of the American Jewish Committee.

He also received the University at Buffalo Chancellor's Medal, the State University of New York Distinguished Citizen Award, the Medaille College Founders' Day Award, the Canisius College Distinguished Citizen Award, and designation as an Outstanding Citizen of the Year by the *Buffalo Evening News*.

He attended Lutheran World Federation conferences in Sweden and Finland. He served two terms on the Executive Council of the Lutheran Church in America after two terms as president of the national church organization's Board of Foreign Missions. He also was elected to the church's Board of World Missions.

He traveled widely throughout the United States, Canada, Europe, and Asia for the church and as a speaker.

He delivered a series of addresses for military chaplains in Germany in 1956. In 1959-60, he gave a series of lectures in Malaya, Hong Kong, and Japan. In 1966, he preached in England and Scotland as part of the British-American Preacher Exchange. In 1986, he traveled with a Chautauqua Institution group to Latvia and the then-Soviet Union.

Born in Columbus, Ohio, he received his bachelor's degree from Capital University in Columbus in 1928.

After graduate work at Ohio State University, he received his Master of Divinity degree from the Hamma School of Theology in Springfield, Ohio, in 1931. Wittenberg University awarded him a Doctor of Divinity degree in 1947.

He served as pastor of Trinity Lutheran Church in Millersburg, Ohio, from 1931 to 1937, then went to Washington, D.C., where he served as associate pastor at the Lutheran church of the Reformation until he became Holy Trinity's fourth pastor in 1944.

"Ralph Loew was a paradigm of virtue, a pillar of wisdom and strength; a devoted, dedicated caring Pastor; a faithful, loving husband; a present and concerned parent; a proud grandfather," said Rev. Charles D. Bang, current pastor at Holy Trinity.

"In addition to these obvious traits, he was a philanthropist of the first order, a generous, grace-filled man who cherished and celebrated knowledge and its pursuit, and who was Christ-like in his devotion to the church and its mission, and, most of all, a man who not only attempted to make that which he touched resemble the vision he had of the Kingdom of God, but who succeeded in doing so."

Surviving are his wife of 57 years, Maxine Uhl Loew; two daughters, Carolyn Engdahl of Northborough, Mass., and Janet Day of Eggertsville; three brothers, Arthur of Sarasota, Elmer of Phoenix, and Erwin of Ocala, Fla; and four grandchildren.

Holy Trinity at worship

The English Evangelical Lutheran Church
of Holy Trinity
1080 Main Street (near North)
Buffalo, NY 14209-2389
(716) 886-2400

At the altar

Dr. Loew and colleagues

with Matthew Winters

Frank Jenson

*Mary and
David
Mumfird*

Charles Bang

117

Dr. and Mrs. Loew

Worship At Chautauqua

I was glad when they said unto me,
"Let us go into the house of the Lord."
Psalm 122:1

Chautauqua, New York 14722

120

Dr. Loew loved his cottage at Chautauqua
summer or winter

Sharing the love of sailing
and music
with family

*Ralph with brothers
Art, Elmer & Erwin*

with Japanese exchange student

123

Back row - l to r
   Steve & Stephanie Engdahl
   Michael & Janet Day
   Jim Day
   Kristin Engdahl
   Lee & Carolyn Engdahl

Front row
   Jennifer Day
   Ralph & Maxine Loew

Ralph & Maxine
Marking 56 wonderful years together